HELSINKI
Birth of the Classic Capital

Jonathan Moorhouse

HELSINKI

Birth of the
Classic Capital
1550–1850

promenades

SKS
Finnish Literature Society
HELSINKI
2003

Suomalaisen Kirjallisuuden Seuran toimituksia 933

Layout: Teresa Moorhouse

paper: Munken Lynx 130g

www.finlit.fi

ISBN 951-746-537-8

Gummerus Kirjapaino Oy
Jyväskylä 2003

Cover: The Cathedral from Tähtitorninvuori (Observatory Hill), Flora Day 2001
Frontispiece: Kaisaniemi, 1830s well-cover, C. L. Engel

CONTENTS

HELSINKI 1808
■ Vanhakaupunki
   (The Old Town)

■ Vironniemi - Kruununhaka
   (The Town's new location)

■■ Sveaborg - Viapori
    Suomenlinna sea fortress

Helsinki plan c. 2000. Early 19th century buildings ▬

Kruunuvuorenselkä frozen bay, looking south to Suomenlinna. 7 Feb. 2001 (+1° c)

Kruunuvuorenselkä ice and Suomenlinna. 3 Feb. 2001 (-21° c)

South Harbour frozen water and islands. 2 Feb. 2001 (-18° c)

Seurasaari 2001

Helsinki region at the end of Swedish rule. The map shows roads over land and i

The north's most important historic route, Kuninkaantie ('The King's Road'), passes the southern coast of Finland and Helsinki. From Viking times it connected western and eastern parts of the Swedish kingdom, from Bergen via Oslo, Stockholm, Maarianhamina on the Åland Islands to Turku (Åbo), Viipuri (Vyborg) and St. Petersburg. Used by kings, couriers, travellers and armies from the 14th century, its rich past threads west and east in rural buildings, mediaeval churches and villages. A short bus journey enables you to sample its picturesque landscape and monuments. To the west Espoon Kartano (Espoo Manor) has Finland's oldest stone arch road-bridge, and nearby is Glims farmstead museum. North, 15 km away is the birth home of Aleksis Kivi the great Finnish playwright, his Taaborinvuori hill, and Nurmi-

THE KING'S ROAD

ɔ from Alanen & Kepsu's Kuninkaan kartasto Suomesta 1776 – 1805

järvi church 1793. In Sotunki, Högberg ridge is Vantaa's highest point. The similar vaults and gables of the 15th-century churches in Espoo, Sipoo and Porvoo suggest that craftsmen travelled along this route. Of interest too is Porvoo's picturesque mediaeval town centre, its graceful Empire style wooden houses and J. L. Runeberg's home. Near Helsinki's Vanhakaupunki is Tuomarinkylä Manor.

In the wild past horses were changed at stage inns and wolves pursued carriages, but even today bears still awake in springtime at Nummi-Pusula,[1] 50 km from Helsinki. Reminiscent of the past are windmills and ancient barns. Distant landscapes of waterfalls and lakes appealed and became immortalised by artists, especially later the views from on high.[2]

Above: Glims farmstead museum, Espoo, 18th & 19th cent. 18 Sept. 2001 (+17° c)
Right: Espoonkartano, (Espoo Manor) bridge (1777). 18 Sept. 2001 (+17° c)

Palojoki, birthplace of Aleksis Kivi (1834 – 1872). Museum. Cottage (1824), living room and oven-bunk. 16 Aug. 2001

Palojoki, Nurmijärvi, birthplace of Aleksis Kivi. From the writer's attic room, harvest time. 21 Aug. 2001 (+18° c)

Palojoki. Aleksis Kivi's Taaborinvuori, the 'swing-pines'. 21 Aug. 2001 (+18° c)

VANHAKAUPUNKI

THE OLD TOWN 1550–1640, VANTAA RIVER MOUTH

HOW TO GET THERE: TRAM 6 TO ARABIA & WALK
BUSES 68, 71, 71V, 73B, VIA HÄMEENTIE
STOPS ANNALA & MUSEUM OF TECHNOLOGY
PROMENADE: 1 ½ HOURS

By the cascading rapids at the mouth of the Vantaa river, the Old Town was founded 1550. Competing with Tallinn for the Hanseatic League and Russian trade, and restricted by a shallow harbour and harsh conditions, the township failed to prosper. In spite of merchants from Porvoo, Tammisaari (founded 1546), Rauma and Ulvila ordered to move to Helsinki, it remained poor as a country village. Anticipating an improved harbour, and prompted by Finland´s Governor General Per Brahe, the township moved to Vironniemi in 1640.

Built west of the river mouth, the Old Town's historic lands survive: a valley, hill and shore, and former 'King's Manor Island' by the rapids. Begin your walk at 154 Hämeentie, Annala Villa (1830s), thereafter stables and grazing Finnish horses lead to the valley. Here the ancient 'Town's Stream' meanders by meadow gardens, and footbridges beckon you to the Vanhankaupungintie road – near the old main square. To the north is the site of the first church, and on rocky Kellomäki hill overlooking forested shores and Hämeentie, is a memorial to Gustavus II Adolphus who convened a Provincial Diet there in 1616.

Around the hill old wooden houses from c. 1800 echo the past. And below the former brick Waterworks buildings c. 1880s, now the Power Station Museum, is the waterfall and Kuninkaankartanosaari. A torrent passes the island on the east side. Upstream the river reflects traditional Finnish country life and is ideal for recreation.[1] Now a rural quarter of Helsinki City, the Old Town with its nature reserve and Viikki arboretum is also an historic gateway to Vantaa, Porvoo and coastal regions.

Annala, Finnish horses in snow. 9 Mar. 2001 (-1° c)

Vanhankaupunginkoski waterfall. Vantaanjoki river. 14 May 2001 (+14° c)

Above: 'The King´s Manor Island'. I June 2001 (+12° c)
Left: 'The King's Manor Island', above waterfall. I June 2001

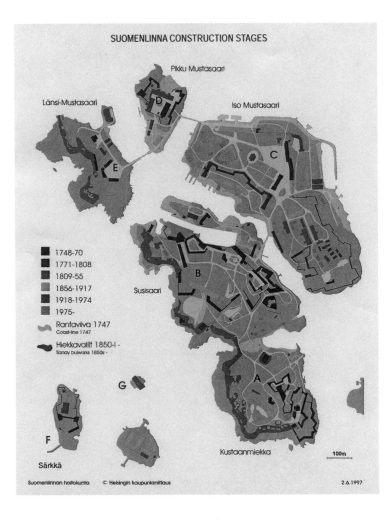

SUOMENLINNA CONSTRUCTION STAGES

Pikku Mustasaari

Länsi-Mustasaari

Iso Mustasaari

D

C

E

Susisaari

B

1748-70
1771-1808
1809-55
1856-1917
1918-1974
1975-

Rantaviiva 1747
Coast-line 1747

Hiekkavallit 1850-I -
Sandy bulwarks 1850s -

G

A

F

Kustaanmiekka

Särkkä

100m

Suomenlinnan hoitokunta   © Helsingin kaupunkimittaus

2.6.1997

SUOMENLINNA

SVEABORG – VIAPORI, SEA FORTRESS, 1748–1808
A.EHRENSVÄRD

HOW TO GET THERE:
FERRY FROM MARKET SQUARE & WATER BUSES 15 MINUTES
JOURNEY. LAUNCH VIA KAIVOPUISTO SHORE TO SÄRKKÄ
PROMENADES: NORTH. 1 ½ HOURS, SOUTH. 2 HOURS

"This really is gods' invention and titans' work. It is terrifying to look at Viapori from the sea. Row upon row of rising granite walls with canon apertures as monsters' gaping jaws ..."[1] reported the former Russian soldier Faddei Bulgarin in 1838. Separated from Helsinki by a bay in summer and joined by an ice road in winter, Viapori was Sweden's Gibralter of the North. It was built to defend the eastern province and bolster morale. Construction began in 1748, the greatest building works then undertaken by Sweden. It was considered unconquerable. The master mind behind the project was an enlightened artillery officer Augustin Ehrensvärd (1710 – 1772), who had studied fortresses in Europe between 1736 – 38. Ehrensvärd was sympathetic to Finland, and was made a Count in 1771 and Field-Marshal 1772.

Seven islands guard Helsinki, and bastions brace the terrain with eight kilometres of granite walls. France formed an alliance with Sweden against Russia, and paid gold to build Viapori (Sveaborg), which grew into a town with professional workers, craftsmen and officers. The greatest work force was 6,750 men in 1751, and in 1805 with 4,600 inhabitants it was Finland's second largest town (Helsinki 4,300, Turku II,300). Built mainly in the 1750s and 1760s Viapori spurred Helsinki's growth and status. Viapori was a fortress, an archipelago fleet base and peacetime garrison. In May 1808 it surprisingly surrendered to Russian forces, who subsequently extended the fortifications. Today Suomenlinna is an outstanding sight, a nature haven and grand architectural ensemble. Amidst its 900 inhabitants are museums, art exhibitions and a summer theatre. It is a unique historical UNESCO world heritage landmark.

ISLANDS Promenades North and South. Fortifications
LÄNSI-MUSTASAARI: Swedish and Russian era. PIKKU MUSTASAARI:
Swedish era and c. 1850. North: ISO MUSTASAARI: Former
garrison town, Swedish & Russian era houses, parade square,
ferry. Kruununlinna Ehrensvärd, Hessenstein fortification.
Suomenlinna Museum - Inventory Chambers, info. South:
SUSISAARI: Tykistölahti, drydock, bastions, Tenaille von Fersen,
Ehrensvärd Museum (1756) and grave. Castle court - outstanding
baroque. KUSTAANMIEKKA: Fortress, bastions, Walhalla restaurant,
The King's Gate 1754, baroque. SÄRKKÄ: Islet, (c.1754), restaurant

Iso Mustasaari (foreground), Susisaari (right), Kustaanmiekka (top right). 29 May 1998 (+17° c)

Iso Mustasaari. Hessenstein fortification (1775 – 1777). 2 Sept. 1994 (+16° c)

Susisaari fortress court. Major's house (1756), and Ehrensvärd´s tomb. 30 Aug. 2001 (+17° c)

Kustaanmiekka. The King's Gate (1754) by Carl Hårleman, steps (1776). 17 Sept. 2001 (+17° c)

Iso Mustasaari. Kruunulinna Ehrensvärd, west wing (c. 1776). 'Devil's Church' banquet hall. 8 May 2002

Susisaari. Tenaille von Fersen (c. 1775), bakery grain store. 6 May 2002

Above: Iso Mustasaari. Kurtiinitalo (1762), stairway (c. 1847). 14 May 2002
Left: Iso Mustasaari. Kruunulinna Ehrensvärd, east wing (c. 1786). 'Ballast Room'. 29 May 2002

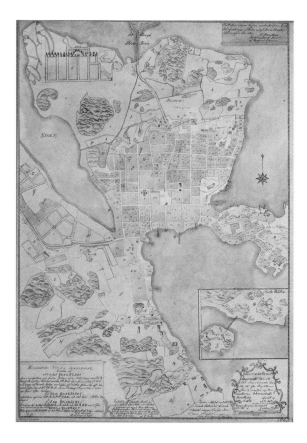

Helsinki. A. E. Gete's map of 1763, revised 1798

VIRONNIEMI

NEW LOCATION FOR TOWN
PENINSULA   1640–1800s

HOW TO GET THERE: TRAMS 1, 1A, 2, 3B, 3T, 7A, 7B
BUSES 16, 17, 18
PROMENADES: TWO, I HOUR EACH

'The Crown's Pasture Land', Kruununhaka, was the first settlement in the new town. Located in Vironniemi in 1640, its hilly terrain was almost surrounded by harbours and a lagoon. Habitation centred on the southern shore, and crossing a new bridge to the north was pasture. Known by its Swedish name Helsingfors, the settlement was little more than a village. Contemporaries observed in 1791: "We assure you that we saw on the streets at least as many cows as passers by."[1] And in 1809 ... "amidst mud were a few streets and red wooden houses. There were only 5 or 6 stone buildings and one church ... and poverty was this town's worst characteristic."[2] However, the construction of Viapori stimulated Helsinki's commerce with the arrival of entrepreneurs, and rich merchants built villas. Visitors were awed by the romantic setting, with great rocks rising from the sea around Viapori.

Gradually the township grew along a north-south orientation with a main square sited close to the present one. The residential blocks too were suitably scaled for horse and cart, and pedestrian life on a hilly terrain, providing a basis for the monumental plan of 1815. In the north-west a public garden by C. L. Engel was begun in 1827, two years later a part was assigned for a University Botanical Garden, and the remainder became a popular landscape garden (1830s). Of renown too was Cajsa Wahllund's restaurant (1828), giving the 'Kaisaniemi' name. A favourite of students and professors, the private tutor Le Duc writes of the early 1840s: "Lunches last up to five or six hours ... For party venues Kaisaniemi was chosen, a charming villa... by the botanical garden and magnetic observatory. There are beautiful paths, wonderful views and a restaurant for relaxing and enjoying tea or coffee."[3]

The first promenade takes us to original rooms in the Kaisaniemi restaurant, and parts of C. L. Engel's Botanical Garden's greenhouses (1832), where blossomed rare plants from St. Petersburg, Tartu (Dorpat) and Turku (Åbo). Fine neo-classical wooden houses (one is now a café) have been relocated by the shore, re-creating the era's particular blend of regular streetscape and informal courts.

A second promenade visits old traditional buildings beyond the classic centre. The Burgher's House, Kristianinkatu 12, is the oldest surviving wooden house in Helsinki on its original site, built c. 1818. Here original interiors can be seen, a rustic court, and wooden lodge-sauna. Maneesikatu 6 is the stone built Old Manège (1830s), opposite J. L. Runeberg's earlier home. See too an idyllic wooden house in the Pohjoisranta 12 sloping court, reminiscent of the past. And near the Pohjoisranta ('North Shore') harbour at Mariankatu 3 is the Old Customs Building in stone c. 1765. Today, the streets and slopes of the coastal areas still reflect the first settlement, and Kaisaniemi's gardens offer a peaceful and verdant haven. The old court forms and harbours still delight the people of Helsinki. Off the Pohjoisranta, ('North Shore'), old sailing barges and schooners are moored, and in the south there are market quays and great public squares.

KAISANIEMI

Helsinki University Botanical Gardens

Greenhouses plans, C. L. Engel	1830
Niche apses in main building	1832
Well-cover, court C. L. Engel	1830s
Garden fence orig. C. L. Engel	1832

Relocated to Unioninkatu

KAISANIEMENRANTA

Neo-classical houses: Helsinki Univ.
in order from Unioninkatu:
r = re-erected ( ) = original location

Bakery r. 1911 (Kaisaniemi)	1843
House café r. 1990 (Uudenmaank. 21)	1823
House r. 1990 (Uudenmaank. 19)	1829
House r. 1990 (Punavuorenk. 23)	1843
Kaisaniemi Restaurant 'Wahlund's'	1839

Bar and cabinet rooms original,
Location in park, by shore & railway

KRUUNUNHAKA

Burgher's House, Kristianink. 12	1818

Helsinki City Museum

Old Manège Maneesik. 6 Jean Wik	1830s

Locations see map. p. 68
Burgher's House is situated topmost
Old Manège is situated upper right

Old Customs Building Mariank. 3	c. 1765

is situated lower right

Kaisaniemenranta. (Left) bakery (1843) and house (1823). 28 June 2001 (+18° c)

Kaisaniemenranta. House (1823), relocated from Uudenmaankatu 21. 9 June 2001

Kaisaniemenranta. Courts. Houses (1829 – 1843). Midsummer eve. 22 June 2001 (+15° c)

Kaisaniemi. University Botanical Gardens. Greenhouses featuring 1830s species
Above: Coffee Arabica. 2 Dec. 2001. Left: cocoa tree. 27 Nov. 2001. Interior (+24° c, hum. 80°)

Above: Kaisaniemi Restaurant. Glazed ceramic tiled stove, salon (c. 1839). 8 June 2001
Left: Kaisaniemi Botanical Gardens. Well cover, C. L. Engel 1830s. 5 June 2001 (+15° c)

Old Manège 1830s Jean Wik, Maneesikatu 6. View from no. 7, J. L. Runeberg's earlier home. 29 July 2001 (+22° c)

Burgher's House (1818), Kristianink. 12, oldest wooden house in city. Helsinki City Museum. 2 Oct. 2001 (+13° c)

Burgher's House (1818), Kristianink. 12, Kruununhaka. Kitchen. 24 Oct. 2001

Burgher's House (1818). Living room. Wooden floors, walls, ceiling. II Oct. 2001

North Harbour, Pohjoisranta, Kruununhaka. Traditional sailing vessels. 20 May 2001 (+9° c)

South Harbour: Schooner Linden (Åland) 26 May 2001 (+9° c). Schooner Kathrina (Helsinki). 2 April 2001 (+6° c)

Helsinki Great Square, early 1800s. Melting snow and ice. 5 Feb. 2002 (+3° c)

HELSINKI GREAT SQUARE EARLY 1800s

Snow sculptures based on the watercolour paintings of 1817 by Carl Ludvig Engel.

This model was located on the same square as today's Senate Square. The church is in its original location in the north west corner. Drawn 5 Feb. 2002 J. L. Runeberg's Day (+3° c). Ice models by Helsinki Master Builders Association and ice sculptors champion.

Helsinki Great Square, early	1800s
Snow and ice model:	
Left: Civic Hall	1804 – 1838
Fore: Ulrica Eleonora Church	1727 – 1827
Rear: Bell Tower	1730 – 1844
Rear: School	1759 – 1840s
Right: Main Guards Building	
Model scale I:5, except Main Guards	
Building which is greater, flame	
oil braziers 180 cm high.	

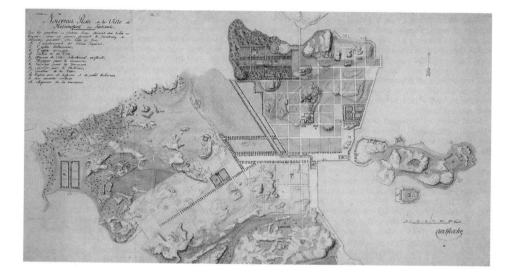

New Plan for Helsinki 1815 – 1816

NEW PLAN FOR HELSINKI

1815 – 1816   J. A. EHRENSTRÖM

ORIGINAL MAP: HELSINKI CITY MUSEUM
SCALE APPROX. I:4000 SIZE 50 x 91
SIGNED A. KOCKE 1815 – 1816[1]

Empire-style Helsinki is the creation of two great talents – the diplomat and courtier J. A. Ehrenström and the architect C. L. Engel. It was the greatest urban building achievement in Scandinavian history, 25 years in the making, and a climax of neo-classical architecture. Devastated by fire in 1808, Helsinki's centre had to be rebuilt for the proclaimed capital of the autonomous Grand Duchy in 1812. Whereas earlier the regional capital Turku (Åbo) was close to Stockholm, Helsinki was chosen by the Tsar for its proximity to St. Petersburg.

Born in Helsinki, Johan Albrecht Ehrenström (1762 – 1847) had travelled in Europe before becoming the town planner and chairman of a new building committee in 1812. On his express wish C. L. Engel was engaged in 1816, one of the greatest architects of the age. The new capital was to be prestigious and monumental, a model city for the empire and symbol of the Tsar. Indeed both Tsars, Alexander I and Nikolai I, admired its architecture and allocated generous funds. The new plan created the structure for the present city and centre. It was built to a magnificent scale. Grand avenues as fire breaks, squares, parks and shores gave birth to a city in harmony with nature, with the great public buildings lining the Senate Square. A grid framed the old centre and new residential areas were related to topography.

Neo-classical architecture, of antique Greek and republican ideals, was the language of the imperial city, representing order and enlightenment. Influential too were the models of St. Petersburg's Italian and French architects and the great classical interpreter Andrea Palladio. And Engel had studied and greatly admired the elegance of Roman and Greek architecture. The new Empire-style Helsinki had the pure expression of a Hellenic city, a town of arcadia. By 1840 it was almost complete with all its houses neo-classical in style. For "The residents of Helsinki, like St. Petersburg, love Greek architecture."[2] wrote Le Duc. Surrounded by rock and water the city was new and gleaming, a 'New Alexandria', with a magnificent heart of columnar buildings and the Senate Square.

Detail: painting 'St. Bernard and Landscape', Gaspar Dughet and Pier Francesco Mola (1612–1666).
Exhibition 'The Art of the Jubilees in Papal Rome 1500–1750'. Amos Anderson Art Museum. 19 Jan. 2001

Johan Sederholm (1722 – 1805) Chapel, C. L. Engel. Old Church Park. 4 Oct. 2001 (+14° c)

Helsinki. View to South Harbour from Suomenlinna. 12 Aug. 1998 (+18° c)

Helsinki. South Harbour, view from Luoto, Klippan. 5 Aug. 1994 (+23° c)

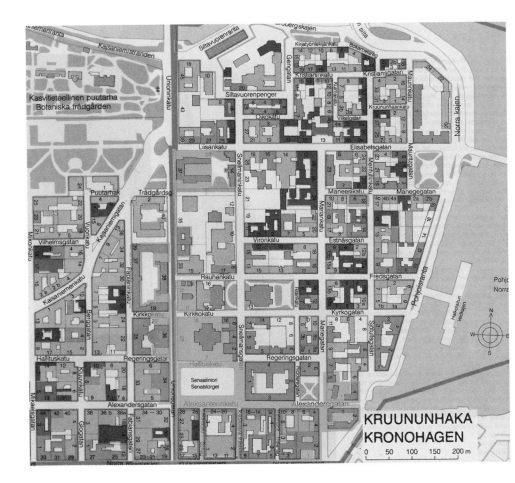

KRUUNUNHAKA
KRONOHAGEN

0   50   100   150   200 m

KRUUNUNHAKA

NEO-CLASSICAL CENTRE
C. L. ENGEL

HOW TO GET THERE: TRAMS I, IA, 3B, 3T, 4, 7A, 7B
BUSES 16, 17, 18
PROMENADES: FOUR, 30 MINUTES EACH, FROM THE
SENATE SQUARE

"Entering Helsinki bay, before us is the unexpected, a marvellous view. Could this town be in Finland, that we used to say was poor? This is a part of St. Petersburg! Except on the right side of the harbour the soaring high rock, the Katajanokka peninsula, which is full of huts - remnants of old Helsinki, reminds me that I am in Finland. Now we are already in the harbour. On the shore a great crowd awaits us, music rings out in the air. We are received like invited guests, ... and the shore hums with life ..."[1]

"The Senate Square is the town's most important place ... Now the rocks have been levelled[2] and the square has a rectangular form. One side of the square has been built of beautiful private brick houses. The huge buildings of the Finnish Senate on the right (coming from the sea direction) and the University on the left fill two sides of the square: the fourth ... will grace not only the town but all Finland[3]... On this gigantic base formed by nature, the cathedral has been erected."[4]

And the guide for this 1838 view was C. L. Engel, the Berlin-born architect who designed almost the whole town.[5] Appointed in 1816 as the architect of Helsinki's rebuilding committee, Carl Ludvig Engel (1778–1840) was a fellow student of his close contemporary the renowned Karl Friedrich Schinkel in Berlin (architect of the Altes Museum 1828). Formerly Tallinn town's master builder (1808) and in St. Petersburg (1815–16), and Turku (1814), Engel excelled in neo-classical architecture; and his drawings won the favour of the Tsar. In masterly simple geometric form and silhouette, and pure archaeological detail, he created harmonic buildings of superb proportion. And as head of the Intendant's office (1824–40) he designed public buildings throughout Finland.

In a letter of 1831 Engel confided: "You cannot imagine how beautiful Helsinki will be, and how beautiful it now is ..."[6] and I consider myself amongst the luckiest, for it is great luck indeed to be able to build whole towns."[7] – Engel wrote in February 1816. Vital too was the transfer of the University to Helsinki in 1828, following the Great Fire in Turku the preceding year. For 'Finland's Tsar Alexander University' had an

continues p. 73   69

Pohjoisesplanadi 11–13, façade (1833) C. L. Engel. 24 Oct. 2001

ALEKSANTERINKATU

2 Main Guards Building C. L. Engel	1840
3 Senate House south wing C. L. Engel	1824
18 Sederholm House, Hki. City Museum	1757
20 Governor General's C. L. Engel	1819
House. Former 'Bock House'	(1762)
Became the town hall	1837
22–28 18th c. rev. C. L. Engel, & J. Wik	c. 1836

POHJOISESPLANADI

I Presidential Palace rev. C. L. Engel	1843
orig. warehouse P. Granstedt	(1814)
3–9 early 19th c. rev. 7 & 3 (Supreme Court)	
11–13 Hotel Societetshuset C. L. Engel	1833
'Seurahuone' orig. facades.	
Helsinki City Hall rev.	1970
15–17, C. L. Engel, 19 (1815) P. Granstedt	c.1830

SNELLMANINKATU

I Senate House drwng. 1818 C. L. Engel	1822
Council of State Palace	

UNIONINKATU

29 The Cathedral St. Nicholas C. L. Engel	
Gt. Church built 1830–40, consecrated	1852
modified: Gt. Steps 1839, pavilions,	
side towers, apostles E. B. Lohrmann	1840s
31 Holy Trinity Church C. L. Engel	1827
33 'New Clinic' hosp. E. B. Lohrmann	1848
34 University Building C. L. Engel	1832
36 University Library C. L. Engel	1840
37 'Old Clinic' hospital C. L. Engel	1833
Univ. Faculty & A. Staubert	1837.
38 Cantonist School milit. C. L. Engel	1823

Right: Detail Plan of Helsinki 1878, Claës Kjerrström

Old Clinic, University Hospital (1833), C. L. Engel & A. Staubert. Unioninkatu 37. 26 July 2001 (+24° c)

important role in the capital, complementing the political-administrative centre with buildings for culture. There are four promenades of the neo-classical centre: the Senate Square, Unioninkatu, Aleksanterinkatu and Pohjoisesplanadi. The following "quotes" are from a summer tour 1838, guided by the architect himself.

First visiting the square "we go inside the Senate House (1822). Its entrance hall is stately and stairway marvellous[8] ... Everywhere is well lit, clean and comfortable."[9] Opposite, "The University Building (1832) is grander and superior ... It is a real temple of knowledge and enlightenment. The entrance hall and stairway would grace Roman palaces."[10] And crowning the square is the Cathedral ... "its rare beauty combines grandeur and great volumes, deriving from the regular plan, proportions, and basic idea."[11] Note too the additions (1840s): side towers, pavilions, great steps[12] and apostle statues.

On ceremonial Unioninkatu street, no. 36 Helsinki University Library (1840) is one of Engel's finest works with magnificent halls, and no. 38 the former Cantonist School (1823) is an elegant composition. Adjoining the University these form supreme neo-classical street architecture. Opposite, no. 37 the first University educational hospital in Finland (1833), no.

31 Holy Trinity Church (1827), and the Cathedral entrance complete this unity.

A stroll on Aleksanterinkatu passes no. 3 the Senate House south wing (1824), once the Intendant Engel's drawing office, and by the shore no. 2 the Main Guards Building (1840). Many of the old brick houses nos. 20 – 28 have façades revised by C. L. Engel, and outstanding is no. 20 'The Governor General´s House' (1819). Helsinki's oldest brick house 1757, no. 18 Johan Sederholm's, is now the Helsinki City Museum of 18th-century culture.

The fourth promenade leads to the Esplanade's north side, pictured in the early 1840s as ... "new charming light coloured houses."[13] Pohjoisesplanadi 11 – 13 is Engel's former noble Hotel Societetshuset (1833). Now the City Hall, with rebuilt interior it once had a "spacious dance hall and beautiful salons."[14] No. 19 now serves Helsinki City Tourist Office, no. 7 the Swedish Embassy's oldest interiors date from 1839, no.3 now the Supreme Court orig. 1816, and no. I the former Tsar's palace (1843) is today the President's, for state occasions. The narrow streets off the Esplanade, particurlarly Sofiankatu a street museum, revive the old town's milieu, and from the market square and harbour we have the magnificent archipelago view.

Senate Square. Left : Senate House (1822), Sederholm House (1757), Gov.–Gen. House (1819). 11 Oct. 2001 (+11° c)

Senate Square. The Cathedral (1852), view from Sederholm House. 1 Oct. 2001 (+9° c)

Senate House (1822), C. L. Engel. Former 'throne room', today's Presidential Reception room. 5 July 2001

Senate House (1822), C. L. Engel. Main stairway, pale green walls, white columns. 9 July 2001

University main building (1832), C. L. Engel. Ionic capital. 4 May 2001 (+15° c)

Senate Square, view to Senate House (1822) C. L. Engel, from University. 24 April 2001 (+10° c)

Above: University (1832). Auditorium cathedra, golden sphinx (1814) from Turku Univ. 30 April 2001
Left: University main building (1832), C. L. Engel. Stairway hall, vestibule. 12 May 2001

Above: Unioninkatu street. Left: University (1832), Library (1840) & no. 38, C. L. Engel. 8 Aug. 1994 (+21° c)
Right: Helsinki University Library (1840), C. L. Engel. Reading hall, fittings (1844). 30 July 2001

Above: The Cathedral, main entrance door handle. 20 Oct. 2001 (+3° c)
Right: The Cathedral, north façade, C. L. Engel. 28 June 2002 (+16° c)

Above: The Cathedral dome, looking north. Consecrated 1852, C. L. Engel. 12 Oct. 2001
Left: The Cathedral crypt, looking east, red brick. Built c. 1830 – 40. 4 Oct. 2001

Above: Sederholm House. Exhib. 'Weddings'. Anna Elisabet Roos, Inkoo vicarage 23.3.1880. 29 Nov. 2001
Left: Sederholm House (1757), Aleksanterinkatu 18. Stairway, stone. 17 Nov. 2001

Pohjoisesplanadi 17 – Unioninkatu 23 (1832, r. 1972), balcony. 14 Oct. 2001 (+9° c)

Pohjoisesplanadi 19 - Unioninkatu 28 (1815), balcony. Pehr Granstedt. 18 Oct. 2001 (+9° c)

Market, harbour view from City Hall, Hotel Societetshuset - Seurahuone (1833). 12 July 2001 (+20° c)

July 1840. The University's great 200 year celebration. The Esplanade, a publication in St. Petersburg

The 'Empire Hall', Governor General's House (1819), C. L. Engel. Aleksanterinkatu 20. 16 July 2001

Banquet Hall (1863) A. H. Dahlström, City Hall. Hotel Societetshuset (1833) C. Ľ. Engel. Pohj.espl. 11–13. 13 July 2001

Above: Sveriges Ambassad, Banquet Hall. Painting Carolus XI Rex Suede, 1696 Klöcker Ehrenstrahl. 28 June 2001
Right: Sveriges Ambassad, Pohj.espl. 7 (1839) A. F. Granstedt, rev. (c. 1923). Cabinet, stove. 29 June 2001

Above: The Presidential Palace. The Great Dining Hall, (1843) C. L. Engel. Pohj. espl. 1. 19 July 2001
Right: The Presidential Palace. The Hall of Mirrors, white walls, gold linings, chandeliers. 18 July 2001

Pohjoisesplanadi 11–13 (1833), no. 7 (1839) & no. 3 (1816) rev. 19 Sept. 2001 (+1

Left: The market and Emperor Nikolai I and Emp

1 The Presidential Palace (1843). 22 Sept. 2001 (+14° c)

ksandra monument (1835), C. L. Engel.

KAARTINKAUPUNKI
GARDESSTADEN

0   50   100   150   200 m

'Smolna', Government Banqueting Hall, the Yellow salon. (1825) C. L. Engel. Eteläesplanadi 6. 6 July 2001

Detail: 'The Market Square, Helsinki Harbour', 1889, Albert Edelfelt (1854–1905). Painting 31x40 cm, Ateneum Art Museum. 4 Jan. 2002

Detail: 'Helsinki from Windmill Hill, Kaivopuisto', 1873. T. Waenerberg (1846–1917). Painting 17x52 cm, Sederholm House. 17 Feb. 2002

Korkeavuorenkatu 19 courtyard. Traditional 19th century wooden buildings. 7 Sept. 2001 (+16° c)

Detail: 'The Liljestrand House' 1862 by Magnus von Wright (1805–1868). Location Kasarmikatu 40. Painting 41x52 cm, Amos Anderson Art Museum. 21 Dec. 2001

Detail: 'Cygnaeus villa' in 1870s (view of South Harbour) 1872 – 74. Johan Knutson (1816 – 1899). Painting 48x77 cm, Cygnaeus Gallery, Kaivopuisto. 16 Feb. 2001

SOUTH & EAST

SHORES, PARKS, RECREATION
KATAJANOKKA, NAVAL BARRACKS
TÄHTITORNINVUORI, OBSERVATORY HILL
KAIVOPUISTO, 'WELL PARK'

HOW TO GET THERE: TRAM 4 TO KATAJANOKKA
AND WALK TO LAIVASTOKATU
TRAMS I, IA, 3B, 3T TO KAIVOPUISTO & TÄHTITORNI
TRAM 10 TO TÄHTITORNINVUORI & BUS 17
PROMENADES: $1/2$ HOUR, $1/2$ HOUR & 1 $1/2$ HOURS

"To the south the sights become freer. All around is an array of beautiful villas ..., here rises the Bathing Establishment, scene of joyful summers, and there the Observatory in whose three towers instruments calculate the heavens; and shipyards resonate, full of action and clatter."[1] Helsinki was busy in the summers when foreign nobility flocked there, especially St. Petersburg families and their entourages, who arrived by steamship from the south harbour to take sea baths in Kaivopuisto.

Nearby, on Katajanokka's northern shore, first visit the former grand Naval Barracks by C. L. Engel, the central seamen's building (1819) admired by Tsar Alexander I; note the officers' 'temple' wings.

The walk south to the favourite recreation land continues from Unioninkatu to the sea, taking in beautiful parks. Tähtitorninvuori hill is graced by C. L. Engel's Observatory[2] (1834) whose astronomical towers overlook splendid harbour views. From here gardens lead down via the Roman Catholic Church (1860) to the former Bathing Suburb.

Kaivopuisto Park, beside Iso Puistotie avenue, with its curved paths for strolling still calls to mind the brilliant carriages and fine dress of Helsinki's Empire period. The Kaivohuone (1838), an enlarged and renowned dance venue, was a popular spa resort for mineral waters; and the former Bathing Establishment (1838) offered baths – warm, cold or with pine-needles. Various delightful villas off old winding roads catch the eye: Itäinen Puistotie 7 Kleineh (1840) by Jean Wik?; Kalliolinnantie 12 'Rock Castle' (1845) by E. B. Lohrmann, with fine harbour views, and no. 8 Cygnaeus Gallery[3] (1869) by J. W. F. Mieritz, on the former Windmill hill.

Today Kaivopuisto's highlight is May Day, a national holiday and great student celebration, and summer nights and autumn evenings.[4] Boats span the brief crossing to the summer restaurant isles of Särkkä, Klippan and Valkosaari; and enjoy concert parties and the sunset views to the Suomenlinna archipelago.

Naval Barracks, Katajanokka. East wing, built to C. L. Engel's (1825) plans 1986. 29 Oct. 2001 (+7°c)

Naval Barracks, Katajanokka. North wing, seamen's (1819), & right (1836), C. L. Engel. 2 May 2002 (+14° c)

The Observatory, Helsinki University (1834), C. L. Engel. Tähtitorninvuori. 25 May 2001 (+8° c)

The Observatory, forecourt residence (1834), C. L. Engel. 18 May 2001 (+10° c)

The Observatory. Revolving central tower, telescope München 1835. 15 May 2001

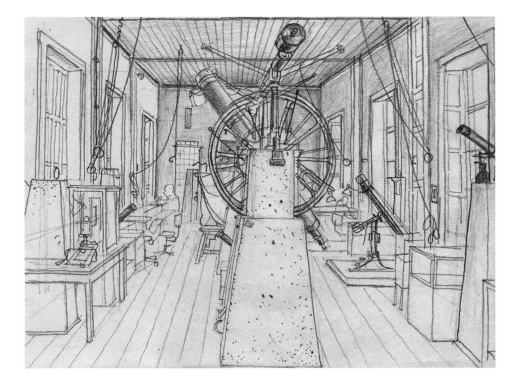

The Observatory, (astronomy & astrophysics) Meridian Hall (1834) C. L. Engel. 16 May 2001

Kaivopuisto park. Above: 25 March 2001 (–3° c), & night party 18 Oct. 2001 (+9° c)
Left: Jetty at site of former Bathing Establishment (1838). 19 Oct. 2001 (+8° c)

Kalevankatu wooden houses, School Museum. Left: no. 43 (1844), 41 (1843), 39 (1840). 19 Sept. 2001 (+16° c)

THE NEW LANDS

PUNAVUORI, KAMPPI, ARCADIA

HOW TO GET THERE: TRAMS TO PUNAVUORI, KAMPPI: 3B, 3T, 6
BUSES 14, 14B, 16
PROMENADE: 2 HOURS

On rough land and rocky slopes, Kamppi, a military 'camp', and Punavuori, the 'Red Mountain', formed new quarters of peaceful garden courts and elegant single storey houses. Here the promenade encounters fine examples and echoes of the early 1800s. At Merimiehenkatu 10 and Uudenmaankatu 38 small wooden houses reflect the artist Magnus von Wright's idyllic scene in 'Annankatu on a Cold Winter Morning.' The painter then lived opposite and near the former home of Engel, with its flower garden and pavilion, at Bulevardi 18 – 20. Le Duc wrote: "How much more pleasant winter is on Helsinki's streets than summer. Soft and even snow falls underfoot; instead of the stumbling horse and cart's painful rattle you hear only the jingling of sleigh bells."[1] The Boulevard leads west to Hietalahti square, the sea and the historic Sinebrychoff park (c. 1830s). Here the family residence of the Sinebrychoff brewery in Bulevardi 40 (1842) – now Sinebrychoff Art Museum – displays old art and the family's Russian Empire-style furniture. By the square is Lönnrotinkatu 37 (1829) by Engel, and Kalevankatu 39, 41, 43 (1840s) wooden houses, now the School Museum.

Welcome to Bulevardi 9 and Café Ekberg. This superb café-pâtisserie, has just celebrated its 150th anniversary. With Parisian and St. Petersburg traditions, the adjoining boulangerie bakes a number of old favourites: 'aleksanteri', 'masariini', 'napoleon', and 'runeberg' tarts. Today 'napoleons' and 'champagne corks' are winners.[2] The Old Church Park and graveyard 1790-1829, formerly Plague Park,[3] is distinguished by Engel's wooden church (1826), the Sederholm Chapel and park gateway. Located on the Boulevard the present park offers rest and reflection amidst its luxuriant trees and gardens.

Notable too on the western shores is Lapinlahti Hospital (1841) and Hietaniemi Old Cemetery[4] (19th century). Helsinki City Museum[5] is housed in the nearby Villa Hakasalmi, built on the virgin lands of Töölö and Arcadia in 1847. Heading north out of the city, past the Kumpula Manor is Kumtähdenkenttä, the site of the Flora Day national anthem celebration.[6]

123

Sinebrychoff brewery estab. 1819. Dray-horses & wagon c. 1900. Bulevardi 44. 20 April 2001 (+4° c)

ANNANKATU	
13 site of painting by M. von Wright	1868
`Annankatu on a Cold Winter Morning'	
BULEVARDI	
18-20 site, wooden house C. L. Engel	1828
his design & home, demolished 1883	
40 Sinebrychoff Art Museum J. Wik	1842
Sinebrychoff Brewery, wooden house	1823
Sinebrychoff Park formed	c. 1830s
KALEVANKATU (Vladimirsgatan)	
39 wooden house School Museum	1840
41 wooden house School Museum	1843
43 wooden house School Museum	1844
LÖNNROTINKATU (Andree gatan)	
37 Finnish Guards hosp. C. L. Engel	1829

MERIMIEHENKATU	
10 E wooden house	19th c.
SALOMONKATU 2 (barracks) bus stn.	1833
UUDENMAANKATU (Nylandsgatan)	
38 wooden house	19th c.
VANHA KIRKKOPUISTO	
Old Church Park, graves	18th, 19th c.
Vanha kirkko Old Church C. L. Engel	1826
Sederholm Chapel, park gate Engel	1828
HIETANIEMI Old Cemetery graves	19th c.
LAPINLAHTI mental hosp. C. L. Engel	1841
KARAMZININKATU (Etu-Töölö)	
2 Villa Hakasalmi Hki. City Museum	1847
KUMTÄHDENKENTTÄ national anthem	1848
KUMPULAN Kartano manor J. Wik?	1841

Right: Detail Plan of Helsinki 1878, Claës Kjerrström

Detail: 'Annankatu on a Cold Winter Morning', 1868 by Magnus von Wright (1805–1868). Location Annankatu 13
Painting 34x53 cm. Ateneum Art Museum. 23 Dec. 2001

Merimiehenkatu 10 E, 19th century wooden house
Two views, courtyard. 7 & 8 March 2001 (-1° c, -4° c)

Above: Sinebrychoff Art Museum (1842), Jean Wik. Top: first main building (1823). 29 March 2001 (+1° c)
Right: Sinebrychoff Art Museum. Oriel window view, Bulevardi 40. 26 Nov. 2000

Sinebrychoff Art Museum. First floor galleries. 28 Nov. 2000

The Sinebrychoff family's Russian Empre style chairs. 30 Nov. 2000

Fredr. Edv. Ekberg's Paris Exp. 1867 porcelain coffee cups. 3 April 2001.
Paris clock and 'Chelsea rabbit' 19th c. 9 Feb. 1997

Café, pâtisserie Ekberg estab. 1852, Bulevardi 9. Mayday pastry, tippaleipä. 26 April 2001

Summer: Vanha kirkkopuisto, (Old Church Park). 'Angel swings'. 26 Aug. 1996 (+18° c)

Winter: Vanha kirkko, (Old Church, 1826) C. L. Engel, and Sederholm Chapel. 9 Feb. 2001 (+1° c)

Kumpula manor (1841), and Vallila allotment gardens. 17 Sept. 2001 (+17° c)

Villa Hakasalmi (1843 – 1847), E. B. Lohrmann. Helsinki City Museum. 29 Sept. 2001 (+6° c)

View NE to Helsinki from Pihlajasaari. 4 August 1998 (+17° c)

View SW to Helsinki from Pyysaari. 16 June 1998 (+21° c)

Kumtähden kenttä, Toukola. Helsinki University Student Union's Flora (flower goddess) day spring celebration.
From 1848 J. L. Runeberg's poem and F. Pacius' music became Finland's national anthem
Vårt land – Maamme-laulu
13 May 2002 (+19° c)

Detail of Ionic capital. 4 May 2001 (+15° c)

By the 1840s the Cathedral rose high above the city, a model city. Helsinki offered a harmonic townscape of low wooden houses and beautiful silhouettes of stone buildings. Engel made the most of the archipelago terrain, building on prominent points to great effect, realising Ehrenström's new town plan with its geometric quarters, avenues and squares. The existing supreme neo-classical centre of elegant columned and regulated structures, has in its entirety and masterly simple geometric forms been an inspiration for classicism, functionalism and modern architecture. Engel's brilliance in proportion and the creative use of the classical vocabulary emulated the greatest architecture of the period. Its magnificent unity provides the heart of the modern city, an ideal city.

Helsinki celebrated the 450th anniversary of its foundation in 2000 (188 years as the capital), accompanied by Stockholm's 750th in 2002, and St. Petersburg's 300th in 2003.

Faddei Bulgarin, *Sotilaan Sydän*. Suomen sodasta Engelin Helsinkiin. Toimittanut ja suomentanut Marja Itkonen-Kaila. SKS, Helsinki 1996. Includes reminiscences of the Finnish War 1808-1809, a summer trip to Finland & Sweden in 1838, and travel observations & impressions from articles, summer 1840.

Louis Léouzon Le Duc, *Pariisista Pohjantähden alle*. Muistelmia Suomesta 1800-luvun alkupuoliskolta. Suomentanut ja toimittanut Marja Itkonen-Kaila. SKS, Helsinki 2001. The basis of this Finnish edition is Léouzon Le Duc's Vingt-neuf ans sous l'Étoile polaire. His works included La Baltique, 1855; Souvenirs et impressions du voyage dans les pays du Nord de l'Europe, 1886. La Finlande 1845 (Vanha Kalevala, 1835, French translation).

C.L. Engel. Kirjeet. Brev. Briefe 1813–1840. Entisaikain Helsinki XII. Toimittaja: Mikael Sundman. Helsinki-Seura Helsingfors-Samfundet. Helsinki 1989.

Helsingin Panoraamat. Kaupunkipanoraamat neljästä tornista kuvattuina. Helsingin Kaupungin Kaupunkisuunnitteluvirasto 1989.

Olof af Hällström, *Matkailijan Suomenlinna.*

Ehrensvärd-Seura ry Suomenlinna 1988.

Kaisaniemi Kajsaniemi. Helsingin Yliopiston Kasvitieteellinen Puutarha. Helsingfors Universitets Botaniska Trädgård. University of Helsinki Botanical Garden. Helsinki/Helsingfors 1998.

Matti Klinge, *A Brief History of Finland.* Helsinki (1981) 1984.

Henrik Lilius, *Esplanadi Esplanaden The Esplanade.* Helsinki, Helsingfors 1984.

Narinkka 1995. Helsinki 1700. Helsingin Kaupunginmuseo Helsingfors Stadsmuseum Helsinki City Museum 1995.

Kalevi Pöykkö, *C. L. Engel 1778–1840.* Helsingin Kaupunginmuseo, Memoria 6. 1990.

Olof Stenius, *Helsingin Asemakaavahistoriallinen Kartasto Helsingfors Stadsplanehistoriska Atlas.* Pro Helsingfors Säätiö/ Stiftelsen Pro Helsingfors. Helsinki/Helsingfors 1969.

John Summerson, *The Classical Language of Architecture.* London (1963) 1980.

Nils Erik Wickberg, *Finnish Architecture.* Helsinki, Finnish edition 1959 (English edition 1965).

ILLUSTRATIONS

Historical maps: by kind permission of Helsinki. DETALJ-PLAN af HELSINGFORS STAD (Detail Plan of Helsinki), Upprättad i öfverenstämmelse med stadens planering och byggnadsart vid ingången af år 1878 af CLAËS KJERRSTRÖM. Prisbelönt, Paris 1878. Helsingin Kaupunginmuseo, Kaupunkimittausosasto.

pp. 28, 34. Kaupunkimittausosasto.

pp. 14, 15, 44. Narinkka 1995 (pp. 206, 207, 272).

pp. 6, 62. asemakaavahistoriallinen kartasto (pp. 69, 74).

p. 93 Bulgarin (p. 262).

p.134 `Angel swings´by artist Kaija Poijula

Maps of quarters: by author & Liisa Valkama.

Drawings: pencil drawings (B) are by the author, drawn on the spot – except pp. 12 & 13 drawn from memory, size A6 148x105 mm.

ACKNOWLEDGEMENTS

I would particularly like to thank the publishers the Finnish Literature Society and the editor Rauno Endén for bringing this book to fruition. I am also grateful to John Calton for kindly reading and improving the text and for her support my wife, art historian Leena Ahtola-Moorhouse.

I am indebted to many people for their generous assistance and in particular to the following: Seurasaari Open-air Museum; Birthplace of Aleksis Kivi, home museum, Palojoki; Nurmijärvi parish; Vanhakaupunki, Annala horses/ Reijo Kuhakoski & cab driver Emma Pembroke; Suomenlinna hoitokunta/ Arja Lukkari; Ehrensvärd Museum; Merenkulkulaitos; Helsinki University, Kaisaniemi Botanical Gardens/ Kustaa Niini, Collections/ Kati Heinämies, Observatory/ Veikko Lind, Main Building, Library; Helsinki City Museum, Burgher's House, Sederholm House/ Marja Nykänen, Kerttuli Wessman; Helsinki City Hall & Gov. Gen. House/ Marja Söderlund; Museovirasto/ Pentti Pietarila; Helsinki Lutheran Church; Marthaförbundet; National Archives, The Council of State Palace (Senate House), 'Smolna', Presidential Palace; The Embassy of Sweden, Ambassador Kerstin Asp-Johnsson & Hans-Ingvar Johnsson, Minister Fredrik Vahlqvist, Ambassador's Secretary Mona Askolin; Art Museums, Amos Anderson, Ateneum, Cygnaeus Gallery, Sinebrychoff; Restaurants, Kaisaniemi, G. W. Sundman; Café Ekberg/ Maj-Len & Otto Ekberg; Ilmatieteen laitos; and Tytti Oukari, Arch.prof. Vilhelm Helander, Arch.prof. Erik Kråkström, prof. Johan Wrede, and Dr. Sirkka Jansson.

NOTES

INTRODUCTION p. 8

[1] Helsingin Panoraamat. An excerpt from Fredrik Berndtson's writing, 1847. The panorama was from Kaivopuisto, Kalliolinna ('Rock Castle') villa, Kalliolinnantie 12.

[2] idem.

[3] idem.

[4] Le Duc, p. 19. And the population rose to 36,350 by 1880. At which point an observer noted " Helsinki has actually grown and developed before our eyes."

[5] Lapland still inspires Finns to view the autumn 'ruska' of russet hues.

[6] Le Duc was the home tutor for Count & Countess Musin-Puškin's Russian-Finnish family of four children, 1842-1844. He was a great cultural friend of Finland, translating both versions of the Kalevala into French, and writing on his time in Finland. He often visited Sweden & Russia. Le Duc, p. 7, 8.

[7] Le Duc, p. 20.

[8] Le Duc, p. 8.

[9] Le Duc, p. 19.

[10] Kenneth Frampton, architectural historian, writing on Helsinki as his ideal city. The Times Literary Supplement, September 18, 1992. p. 12.

[11] Le Duc, p. 255.

THE KING´S ROAD p. 14

[1] First traces, 28 March 2002. STT, H.S. 1.5.2002.

[2] Inspired by J. L. Runeberg & Z. Topelius.

VANHAKAUPUNKI p. 28

[1] Pirunkallio-Tuomarinkylä river banks: picnics, cycling, canoeing, bathing and horse riders.

SUOMENLINNA p. 34

[1] Bulgarin, p. 177.

VIRONNIEMI p. 44

[1] Narinkka 1995, p. 199 French émigré Count Alphonse Fortia de Piles. Inhabitants then numbered about a 1000.

[2] Bulgarin, p. 182.

[3] Le Duc, p. 138.

NEW PLAN FOR HELSINKI p. 62

[1] Helsingin Asemakaavahistoriallinen Kartasto. N:o 74.

[2] Le Duc, p. 119.

KRUUNUNHAKA p. 68

[1] Bulgarin, p. 178.

[2] Bulgarin, p. 182. "Now granite knolls and entire rocks have been exploded on a grid to form streets, squares and building sites, ..."

[3] Bulgarin, p. 182.

[4] Bulgarin, p. 183.

[5] Helsinki City Museum, Exhib. Sofiankatu. 'New Alexandria'. "Engel planned more than 30 public buildings in Helsinki and supervised the construction of over 600 dwellings."

[6] C. L. Engel. Kirjeet, p. 276

[7] C.L.Engel. Kirjeet, p.44

[8] Bulgarin, p. 183.

[9] Bulgarin, p. 185.

[10] Bulgarin, p. 185.

[11] Bulgarin, p. 183.

[12] Replacing Engel's Main Guard colonnade (1819). Additions: architect Ernst Bernhard Lohrmann (from Berlin).

[13] Le Duc, p. 246.

[14] Le Duc, p. 85.

KAARTINKAUPUNKI p. 102

[1] Le Duc, p. 254.

[2] Le Duc, p. 246.

[3] Le Duc, p. 250.

[4] Le Duc, p. 250.

[5] Rights 1743, King Fredrik I; now in October.

[6] Le Duc, pp. 24, 25.

SOUTH & EAST p. 112

[1] Le Duc, p. 20.

[2] Engel's first commission in Finland was Turku Observatory (1819).

[3] Villa housing the Finnish art collection of Fredrik Cygnaeus (1807–81).

[4] From hot air balloons, kites, sunbathers to snow white hares & toboggans.

Naval Barracks C. L. Engel 1819, 1836, (1986) Merikasarmi, Laivastokatu. Former hospital, opposite barracks, A. F. Granstedt 1838. Ministry of Foreign Affairs. Tähtitorninvuori Observatory C. L. Engel 1834, Helsinki University, Kopernikuksentie. Kaivohuone (spa), Iso Puistotie I, orig. C. L. Engel 1838.

[1] Le Duc, p. 248.

[2] Today´s winners are also Tobogganing Day and May Day specials, and fine breads.

[3] Where many Helsinki victims were buried in 1710.

[4] Tram 8.

[5] Trams 4, 7, 10.

[6] Tram 6, the leading act in 2002 was the rock band 'Cleaning Women'